I0445576

7 WAYS

TO LIVE

IN-JOY

TODAY

KATHLEEN IVES

Copyright © 2025 by Kathleen Ives

ISBN 979-8-9993873-0-1 (Paperback Edition)

ISBN 979-8-9993873-8-7 (Hardcover Edition)

ISBN 979-8-9993873-6-3 (E-Book Edition)

August 13th, 2025

Kathleen Ives

7 Ways to Live IN-Joy Today

All rights reserved.

No portion of this book may be reproduced in any form without written permission from the publisher or author, except as permitted by U.S. copyright law.

For Marni.

My sunflower gal, thank you for shining your sun on us.

Love you, forever.

About the Doors

· · · ● · ● ● · ·

L ife is all about the doors we choose to walk through. Some open easily. Some close without warning. And just when we think we've run out of options, a new door appears.

This book is made up of seven doors. Each one leads you somewhere new, though where you go is entirely up to you. There is no right order. No locked rooms. Just invitations. You might walk through one and stay a while, or open it, take a look around, and gently close it again. All of that is allowed here. You are the one with the key. And wherever you choose to begin, I trust that it's exactly where you're meant to be.

What's Inside

Why You? Why Now? Why Me?

• • • ● • ● • • •

There are millions of people struggling with their mental health in our world today. There's also an endless supply of self-help and happiness-promising books that will tell you to take a hot bath, wake up at 5am, go for a walk, eat more kale, do a cold plunge, and meditate.

This is not one of those books.

Now, all of those things *will* provide a supportive environment for experiencing joy, but the real joy comes from with-IN. You can do all the healing modalities there are, but if you don't shift your internal environment—it will never reflect your external.

In case nobody has told you lately, or ever, you deserve to be able to feel joy—and joy doesn't have to be far away. Life is not about suffering and heartache. It's about learning and experiencing.

Shifting your mindset in small, easy-to-digest ways will add up to large changes in your overall well-being. I know, because I have done it. All of the tips, lessons, stories, and modalities in this book I have personally used to pick myself up out of a well of darkness and live my most joyous life. I hope at its very core, this book inspires you to see yourself the way others see you, the way I see you, full of light and with plenty of love to give and receive.

I heard an analogy of a sunset one day that I like to apply when I need to dig for a little more kindness for myself. When you look at an awe-inspiring sunset, it's so beautiful it stops you in your tracks. You want to savor the moment, so you pull out your phone and snap a photo (now I realize if this book stands the test of time, and you're reading this 100 years from now, you will probably not know what a phone is and be able to blink and save memories to your brain or something but, nonetheless here we are now glued to our smart phones in 2025).

Never once has someone looked at the photo of the sunset and thought, "Wow, this is way prettier than the real thing." It is always more beautiful in real life, being experienced in its full feeling and color. I want you to start thinking of yourself as that sunset. Every time you think you aren't good enough, or you look bad in a photo, or you aren't where you thought you'd be in life by now, remember you are a sunset. Unfortunately, you only get to see yourself as the photograph, whereas everyone else gets to witness and experience you like a real-time sunset. You are far more magical than you think you are, I promise you that.

Three years ago, I was in a 10-year relationship, had a beautiful home and dog, lived in a suburb in Colorado, and worked my dream positions in corporate marketing; from the outside, it looked like I was really happy. It seemed I had it all together. My life could have been someone else's dream life. At one time, it was even mine.

But I couldn't shake an intuitive feeling deep in my heart that this wasn't my life. I started to feel guilty for feeling like I wanted more. More in my career. More in my partner. More in my life. Who was I to want more? More than this?! How dare I? There are people suffering all over, so I should be grateful for my cushy life and be done with it. Yet, the intuitive feeling kept pouring over me. Why wasn't I happy? Why wasn't this enough? What was wrong with me?

When we aren't willing to make changes ourselves, the universe will often give us a nudge. Sometimes that nudge feels more like a push down a flight of stairs, and it's rarely comfortable. My nudge came with the death of my soul dog, Lilly. She was my everything. I adopted her as a senior dog, and she brought me more love and companionship than I ever thought possible. She took so much of my suffering from me and stabilized our household so many times. She truly was an angel, not a dog. Tears well in my eyes to this day as I write, thinking about the pure and unconditional love she gave to me, so willingly.

When I found out she had cancer, it broke me. For the first time in my life, staring death in the face and the loss of that attachment to my safety blanket hit me excruciatingly hard and I felt like I couldn't take a full breath. I was grieving her before she was even gone. I knew I couldn't go on like this, and I had to find a way to survive without her.

A problem solver to my core, I started researching and trying all different modalities to deal with grief, trauma, loss, and death. I started journaling, I started doing breath work, and I spent more time outside. These all helped immensely, but the words I spoke to myself were the most important. I would tell myself every single day, "You are going to be okay, you can and will get through this. You can get through anything." I would repeat them subconsciously when I would feel panic, and it soothed my heart.

As I became more comfortable with the heaviness, it was really just a comfort I found in myself.

Eight short weeks later, was Lilly's day to cross the rainbow bridge. The day I had dreaded for years and couldn't even think about, had surprisingly turned out to be one of the most beautiful and awe-inspiring days I've ever experienced. The connection we had from the moment I opened my eyes that morning, and just knew, to the hours we spent laying in the grass together just loving on each other, to her last moments were some of the deepest expressions of love I've ever felt. In fact, my partner at the time and I even went to get ice cream after the nurse left, and Lilly sent us two signs on the drive there, letting us know she's still with us. I always say Lilly's greatest gift to me was her passing, as the lessons I learned from it lit a fire of confidence in my soul that I desperately needed to burn.

Now I know starting out a book about experiencing joy with the death of a dog is not the most conventional opener, but stick with me,

I promise it's actually two sides of the very same coin.

The more I allowed all feelings to come through instead of bottling them up or pushing them away, the more at peace I was. It's like I was driving a car and my emotions were in and out of the back seat being rowdy at different times. As long as I allowed them in the car, but did not let them drive, eventually they would always settle down. It's when I didn't allow them in the car at all, that both mental and physical problems arose. This state of allowing not yet full-blown joy, but allowing, started to create space for magic. Remember how I said I wanted more out of life? Allowing that feeling to sit in the car with me made it less scary and I felt less guilt towards it. We got more comfortable with each other as time went on.

Fast forward 8 months, and I was living in Los Angeles, CA, having been relocated for my dream job offer working in the beauty industry. I was following my intuition more now, but still not entirely whole-heartedly. I had a tugging feeling

I was supposed to live my LA chapter alone, but it seemed terrifying and daunting to think about separating from yet another deep attachment in such a short time period. I had never been alone. I'm an only child, and after I had lived with my parents, I lived with roommates or friends, then with my partner. I had never even spent more than one or two nights alone in my life, and I had my dog Lilly at the time so I was truly never alone alone (now, you're never truly *alone*, but that's another book—I won't scare you off just yet). I just couldn't shake that feeling. Each day that passed where I didn't listen to it, more things would happen in an attempt to show me that this wasn't my best path. We do have free will, and I'm sure some version of me would have stayed on that path out of fear, but not this version.

Finally one day, actually Valentine's Day to be exact, since apparently my soul enjoys dark humor, I just couldn't do it anymore. I got the strangest ball of courage out of nowhere and just blurted out the most honest thing in my heart.

I knew deep down I was never going to have the capacity to grow on the path I wanted in my current partnership. I spent years feeling guilty for knowing that, and explaining it away with genuine hope, out of love. It wasn't fair to either of us, and from that day forward I vowed to myself I would always follow my intuition, making love-based decisions, not fear-based decisions.

That dedication to love-based decisions removed any regret or resentment from my prior relationships and interactions and gave me a new sense of peace. Little did I know, it would also set me on a rollercoaster of life experiences over the next three years that would change the course of my existence forever, and my ability to be happy and find joy—in any environment or situation.

Want to know the best part? You have the exact same ability. I'm no doctor, I'm not a therapist, I don't have a massive following or any fancy credentials to prove to you that on paper I must know what I'm talking about. What I am though, is I AM you. I see you, I feel you, I likely have been where you are now in some relational capacity, hoping for more out of life. I am here to mirror to you that you do have the power to change your life as I did—with no fancy tools—just big dreams, a big heart, and determination, fueled by exhaustion with what is and hope for the future.

Door 1: Open Your Heart to New

• • • ● • ● • ● • •

I hate to break it to you, but the #1 thing keeping you from experiencing joy RIGHT now, is you.

We all have a collection of beliefs, habits, and ideals we've picked up along the way from our environment and upbringing that shape how we view our realities. Each individual is going to view life differently. The key is in being open to possibilities. Lessening the grip on what we think we know, making room for different perspectives and ways to solve problems. When you open your heart, it's scary. It's vulnerable. Much like falling in love, it can be terrifying. If you shut yourself off from it out of fear though, you will never get to experience the magic of an open heart.

Think about when you were a child, whether you experienced trauma or not, you had an innate sense of wonder. That wonder and curiosity is what let your mind expand to experience more magic in life. Children are often more creative, better problem solvers, and much happier than adults. I know you're thinking, well of course, they don't have bills to pay and responsibilities, which is true, but they also have a mindset that we could take notes from and apply to our adult lives. The anxiety of adulthood would feel a little less heavy.

I like to think of life as a soul school, and we get to create whatever reality we wish to live in. We arc all creators, and we are all creative in some capacity or another. The more open-minded and open-hearted you are, the more capacity for expansion you have. I know, that got a little woo woo there but I mean it. Even if you think someone is crazy for believing something that may be a little too out-there for you, if they aren't hurting anyone and even perhaps thriving due to that belief, what is the downside of giving something new a try if what you're working with isn't working well for you anyways?

We often judge others for their lifestyle choices, beliefs, appearance, and decision-making processes, even when the ones we have chosen really aren't doing much for us. I encourage you to slow down and really read this book with an open mind, an open heart, and the openness to accept a different perspective into your life. If nothing else, the sheer ability to accept perspectives in contrast to your own without getting triggered or angry is a feat in itself.

I have struggled my whole life to finish books cover to cover. I would always pick up a book, read pieces and parts, and then put it down and come back to it. I have a whole bookshelf of mostly-read books with only a few fully completed. I used to shame myself for this reading style, but then I realized that it was perfectly okay and that I was absorbing what I needed in whatever time frame I was supposed to. My point being, I specifically designed this book to be unintimidating in length (only time that's a plus) so that you would be able pick it up and read any section you feel you were called to. We have enough pressure in our lives—reading a book should not be another one. A good rule I like to follow in any situation is to take whatever resonates with you, and leave whatever doesn't. You get to choose what you take with you and what you leave. I invite you to blow the lid off of what you've been conditioned to think you 'should' be doing, and have the courage to pave your own path even in the very smallest of ways.

In order to accept joy (yes, some of you are currently actively rejecting it) you must stretch your heart a little. I promise you your heart has the capacity for it. There is no shortage of joy. It is safe to feel joy. You are safe to feel joy. In fact, you are safe to FEEL, anything. There is an entire ocean full of love and joy all around us, but it is up to YOU and you only to decide what size container you want to bring to the shoreline to fill up.

Opening your heart to change is the key. The only constant in life is change. The more we accept and even come to appreciate that fact of life, the more in flow we become. You may be thinking, "What does it even mean to be *in flow*?" Think of your life as a river. Your environment is your emotions—is it raining on the river? Is it sunny? Is it cold or warm? These emotions (much like the weather) can change often and can sometimes bring obstacles into the river like a few fallen branches we have to deal with.

Now in your river there are these fallen branches, along with some logs floating around, a few boulders, maybe some rocks, trash, and other items blocking the flow of water. Think of these items as your experiences and traumas. Every river is going to have a few rocks. It's up to you to clear the path as best you can so water can still run through the river. Some rivers have fallen tree trunks bobbing on the surface, but still flow beautifully. It's not about clearing everything out of your river, but finding YOUR flow. We all have our own current, which is ever-changing with time and age.

What being truly *in flow* means to me, is keeping my river free of as much debris as I can while accepting and building around any fallen trees and recognizing the current will never stop: no matter what speed, it will ALWAYS flow. The less debris I have, the easier it will flow. The more obstacles I can accept and create around, the easier it will flow. I can mentally handle the cold of the river, knowing that it will warm up with the change of seasons. Everything is temporary. Surrender to that, and you will find yourself *in flow*.

Changing the flow of your life is like learning choreography to a new dance. You don't learn all the steps at once. Here's a little mental trick I use when I want to make some changes in my life but feel overwhelmed thinking about all of them.

Let's call it The 5, 6, 7, 8 Method:

For any dancers, I'm sure you can already hear the rhythmic pattern being shouted in your head. For my non-dancers, whenever you start a dance, the instructor usually claps with each number out loud and yells 5, 6, 7, 8... as your cue to begin the choreography. We're going to use this analogy to implement positive new habits into your life and make them stick.

5, 6, 7, 8... here is your first step. This could be going to bed an hour earlier, smoking one cig a day instead of two, eating a vegetable with dinner, not texting them back—whatever it is, choose something small. Do that first part of our choreography for 2 weeks until you feel like you've got it down.

Now we add another step to the dance. These steps might include getting some daily sunshine, or going for a walk. Something you can add on to our first bit of choreography so we're practicing two new things now. Piece these together for 2 more weeks.

Another one. Now originally, this piece of choreography may have seemed too intense to do right off the bat or too great of a change to take on, but now since you already have 2 other pieces of the dance down, it doesn't seem so scary, does it? You're ready! Add this in and do all 3 moves for 2 more weeks until you've got it down. By now you've been doing the first new habit for 6 whole weeks! Congrats.

I'm sure by now you're catching on to the new pattern here. When we break down change into tiny, bite-sized steps instead of a whole dance, you can learn the choreography to your new life in a much easier way, and it will likely be a lasting change in flow.

How beautiful life can be.

How beautiful, so can death.

How beautiful other lives have been,
and will be.

NOTES

I wanted to leave some blank lined pages in between chapters in case there were any notes or thoughts or ideas coming to mind that you wanted to jot down while you read. Think of it like a little scratch pad or journal. If that doesn't feel good to you, then use it to write your grocery list or doodle or make a paper airplane or write your number down to give to the cutie at the coffee shop next to you.

This is YOUR book, do with it what feels right to you.

• • • ● • ● • • •

Door 2: Visualization

• • • ● • ● • • •

N ow, I know I told you I wouldn't make you meditate, but there are certain aspects of meditation that will greatly assist you in activating your inner joy. Stay with me here—I promise I won't have you chanting ohms or sunning your bumhole or putting any quartz crystals in any precarious places or anything like that (that'll be the next book).

One of those aspects is the power of visualization. We all have an inner movie theater in our mind that is constantly playing films. Sometimes those films can be horror films, sometimes drama, sometimes comedies. What we often forget is that we own the theater—and get to decide which showings we attend. Even if a horror film is playing in theater #4, we can choose to watch the comedy in theater #6. It doesn't mean that the horror film isn't playing in theater #4, it just means we are not focusing so much of our attention on it. Energy flows where focus goes. Acceptance over avoidance.

I want you to try an exercise with me:

Close your eyes if you safely can.

Take 3 deep breaths. With each breath, first fill up your belly with air, then fill up and expand your chest, and then pause briefly at the top before letting all the breath go (bonus points for an audible exhale: let that shit GO).

You can breathe normally now, however feels comfortable, and I want you to use your imagination and start to visualize a glowing orb of yellow light in your belly (I know, I know—cue eye roll, but stay with me, people!).

With each breath in, the light around this glowing orb is going to grow bigger, and wider; try to feel it expanding inside of you.

Now look into this glowing orb like it's a crystal ball playing a movie for you. The scene is you, a version of you that is experiencing joy in whichever way you would like. Think about a time you were so joyous and having a great time, and replay that memory into the orb. If you can't think of a time you felt joy, that's okay too! That's why we're here. In that case, use your imagination to think of a version of you without restrictions or barriers to joy. What would you be doing? Where would you be? Try to project that version of you onto your orb screen and watch what plays out. Shoot for the stars, it doesn't need to feel attainable right now.

Okay, I'll pause here. I realize I'm telling you to close your eyes and also read at the same time and we haven't gotten to that level of wizardry yet, so take a moment for the orb exercise here.

As you finish watching the joyous you in your orb screen, take a moment to recognize any shifts or changes in how you feel—right now, in this moment. Do you feel lighter? Perhaps even a bit emotional? Nostalgic? You might even catch a smile forming across your face. Acknowledge whatever is coming up for you and let yourself feel it. How does your body feel right now? Allowing yourself to feel is one of the more major accomplishments and courageous things in our world you can do right now. Some may even argue it's a glorious act of rebellion.

I really want to hone in on the fact that feeling your feelings is not weakness. I'll repeat that. FEELING YOUR FEELINGS IS NOT WEAKNESS. Okay, that was a little louder than intended, but I am deeply passionate about this! It's actually the opposite of weakness. Allowing the ability to feel your feelings, knowing that you can handle and release ANY pain that may come up, is true courage and strength. Scream crying into a pillow is strength. Yelling alone into an open field is strength. Sitting in discomfort is strength.

People always say things like "be strong" or "don't cry" or "suck it up." If you truly break down what those sentiments actually mean at a core level, what the person is telling you is, "Hey, how about you bottle up those emotions instead of releasing them in a healthy way, because releasing them never felt mentally or physically safe *to me*, so I am now unconsciously projecting that onto you to try and protect you since I have always been afraid of whatever pain I may feel or what people may think about what I am feeling. So in order to reject judgment and pain, I compartmentalize my feelings and ignore them as a defense mechanism. Since I've been doing this with my own feelings for a long time, I also don't know how to handle your feelings either." Hence, the "suck it ups" and the "don't crys." Sound familiar? Feeling a little parental trigger? I get it.

Let's go back to the sentiment that forgiveness is for you, not for them on this one. I've found that healing yourself and living your truth can actually influence the people around you far more than trying to tell them how to heal. Be the living breathing example, not the infomercial. I've led many a horse to water, I've even dunked a few heads under, but unfortunately the horses I tried the hardest with remained dehydrated. People will only change if they want to, not because *you* want them to. Oof, now take a drink of water for that pill we just dry-swallowed.

Back to the beautiful, glowing golden orb version of you we just visualized. I want to let you in on a little secret: this joyous version of you already exists. This version of you IS you, which is why you're able to feel it, even if you think you just made it up. Might I add, your imagination is the most powerful tool you have. Look around you. Everything you see was once a thought. The bus station, the couch you may be sitting on, cars driving by, your clothes, even this very book, was once a thought before it was materialized.

Your mind can create entire belief systems, which you can also use as tools to create whatever reality you want to live in. Every single human on this planet is viewing reality differently. Each individual's view of reality comprises their personal experiences, memories, emotions, traumas, personality traits, and perception of time. No two humans have the exact same experience, and we often spend tireless hours trying to make others see the world the way we see it—usually to no avail—instead of accepting the differences and acknowledging that we truly are all stars of our very own unique reality tv shows (which we are also all executive producers of).

When in doubt remember:

Delulu is the Solulu.

NOTES

If you don't use this as a grocery list or a love note and would like a journal prompt, I've got one for you:

What are 3 limiting beliefs I hold about myself that are currently restricting me from experiencing joy?

• • • ● • ● • • •

Door 3: Reflection

• • • ● • ● • • •

W e often hear the word *gratitude* thrown into many different arenas these days, and although it's having quite the trending marketing moment complete with t-shirts, journals, and other HomeGoods-esque merch, in its essence, true gratitude is the foundation for an internal mindset shift.

In order to learn to feel gratitude—not just say it, but FEEL it—you must first train your body to learn it is safe to feel. Our egos inherently try to keep us alive. They are not evil or bad, we need them to survive, but they have a way of trying to protect us that isn't always for our highest good. As part of human nature, we rarely do anything that isn't self-serving in some way. Now you may be thinking, "Kathleen, I am always giving to others. I never do anything for myself.

I don't self-serve." Think about it from a deeper layer. You over-giving to others instead of filling up your cup first makes you feel needed. It makes you feel like you're contributing in some way to someone else's happiness or care—which in turn makes you feel like you're a good person. Perhaps you have a wound or a trigger that allows you to believe that if you do anything for yourself first, that would make you a selfish person or that if you're not serving others all the time, then you aren't worthy of love. That simply just isn't true. You cannot pour from an empty cup.

I'm sure some of you think you have to earn people's love and affection and you aren't inherently worthy of it just for existing and being you. Sorry to burst your bubble, my loves, but unfortunately what we have been conditioned to believe about our worth is stained with years of confusion, agendas, insecurities, and fear. If you are here, on this planet, reading this book right now, I'm here to tell you that you (yes, you!) are WORTHY of love.

Let that sit for a second. Let it sink in.

How does that feel in your body? Some emotions may come up, and that's okay. It could be relief, sadness, joy, anger, doubt, fear, happiness, love, or even a smoothie of them all. Don't fight them, just let them be. Acknowledge them with curiosity over judgment. Sometimes it's helpful to even say hello to those emotions coming up and ask them what they are here to say or teach us. I PROMISE you without a shred of doubt, thinking about feeling your emotions is way harder than actually feeling and moving through them. That is because when we *think* about feeling them, we're in our heads, coming from a fear-based state, whereas actually *feeling* them is coming from our heart space, a love-based state. Yes, crying and screaming into a pillow can be from a love-based state. Courage is love. The courage it takes to feel and release something is love. Look at you, already feeling a little more love today! Proud of you.

Life comes at you fast, and we don't always want to reflect on the past for varying reasons. We live in a world of "keep it goings" "move it forwards" "walk it offs" and "suck it ups." Some aspects of your experiences may be painful, and difficult to want to reflect on. If we take our human emotions of anxiety and fear out of the equation, the ability to feel and reflect on any event in our lives is not harmful. In fact, internalizing it and not letting yourself feel it can lead to more anxiety, physical and mental pain, and disease. When you internalize suppressed emotions, your body stores that energy instead of releasing it. Pent-up stored energy of this nature can grow and grow in your physical body until you are living in a state of stress, fight-or-flight, and dis-ease. Which, you guessed it, can cause disease.

Now that we've gotten a little more comfortable learning to feel, let's get into the magic. The way our bodies and souls communicate what we want or need is through feeling. Before you say "I'm hungry," you felt hunger in your belly. Before you say "I love you," you felt a warm wash of love for someone. Before you say "I'm freaking out," you probably felt your heart beating faster and breathing increased. Energy flows where your focus goes. If you focus on negatives, you will attract more negative experiences. If you focus on positives, you will attract more positive experiences. This is not a woo-woo concept, just a universal fact of energy. The more we can break down the mental barriers to ideas that seem "weird" or "too spiritual" or just generally uncomfortable—and remember that the concepts I am explaining here are actually just universal human-energy connection concepts—the easier it will be to digest. You don't need crystals and sage to do any of the work I am proposing here.

Reflecting on our experiences in life, including our traumas, and searching for a lesson or a positive in them is one of the healthiest games you can play. It may be difficult at first, but with time, instead of trying to find a needle in a haystack, you will see more clearly and be able to look at your experiences in an entirely new light.

I'll use my own personal experience as an example, and you will see two very distinct perspectives on how to look at the events that have transpired over the last 3 years of my life. The first way, I will explain from a place of fear and lack. Let's call her Doubting Darla. The second, I will explain from a place of love and courage. Let's call this perspective Courageous Kath. Cheesy, I know, but it will prove my point.

Here are a few very true events from the last 3 years of my life from Doubting Darla's perspective:

- I left a 10-year relationship without ever living alone before and had to fully support myself, had no partner, and was alone

- My soul dog died and my comfort was stripped away, and I had no more companionship

- I was living in a new city with a new job and new responsibilities and was completely overwhelmed and had no idea what I was doing

- I was terrified to drive and got in a couple accidents which made me want to drive even less

- My father's dementia keeps getting worse and he forgets that I was his daughter most of the time

- I got laid off from my job with no notice, after building a marketing career for 10+ years

- I've been dealing with awful gut health issues and terrible acne

- I've lost friendships with people who no longer resonate with me

- I was single for nearly 3 years

- My apartment flooded and I lost a ton of items and my living space was under reconstruction for nearly a year

- One of my best friends died of ovarian cancer very suddenly

Now here are those same incidents from Courageous Kath's perspective:

- I left a 10-year relationship without ever living alone before and was given the opportunity to learn about my own independence and strength for the first time in my life

- My soul dog died and taught me crucial tools to help with deep grief that I now share with others

- I was living in a new city with a new job and new responsibilities and pushed myself to overcome obstacles and learn new skills and gain knowledge and experience

- I overcame my fear of driving on the highway (yes highway, not freeway LA, people) and although I got in a couple accidents I was protected from being hurt and I am okay

- My father's dementia is progressing, and now I see how the power of loving energy ties us together stronger than any relationship label ever could

- I got laid off from my job after building a marketing career for 10+ years, and it was the nudge I needed to focus on what truly makes my soul feel aligned; it gave me the opportunity to live without a blanket of stress to figure it out safely and calmly

- I've been learning so much about gut health and skin and how I can support it to be the healthiest version of myself

- I've allowed friendships to fall away, with people who are on different paths, without letting love for their individual journeys go

- I have had the gift of learning to love who I am without a partner for nearly 3 years and was able to discover new layers of who I am and what I like

- My apartment flooded and I was able to purge items I no longer needed and looked forward to an entirely new feel to my space (whilst not having to pay rent for nearly a year)

- One of my best friends is now my most powerful guardian angel, guiding and protecting me and teaching me how to see the signs and follow my heart

These are the exact same events, experienced from two completely different realities. One mindset is going to keep you feeling stuck, small, helpless, and overwhelmed. The other is going to make you feel strong, empowered, grateful, and loved. Red pill or blue pill, the choice is yours.

Release the fear of change, for no matter what mountains you have to climb, things are always working in your favor—*for* you, not *to* you.

Recognize and appreciate the magic of the process.

NOTES

You know the drill.

Prompt: Write out 5 things that have happened to you in your lifetime from each of those dual perspectives of Doubting Darla and Courageous Kath—one side skewing negative, one side skewing positive.

I promise you can find the positive in even the darkest of traumas. You may be surprised what positives you've taken from seemingly negative experiences.

• • • ● • ● • ● • • •

Door 4: Detox from the Shoe Drop

• • • ● • ● ● • • •

W e all have a lovely way of putting up blocks and barriers to joy because joy can feel really scary to many people. Often, when you are experiencing joy, your ego wants to protect you and comes up with scenarios and false crises of impending doom that make you believe that there's no way this feeling can last a long time. So you shift into a state of anxiety, waiting for the other shoe to drop.

Sound familiar?

Well, I was right there too. That's why I'm here now to help you detox from the shoe-drop mindset.

I was stuck in a pattern of believing I wasn't good enough, smart enough, thin enough, successful enough, or worthy enough to experience long-lasting joy. Sure, I had great times and fun experiences, but I never thought that it was sustainable. I would get that wave of fear when things were going well, that the ride down the hill was coming and it was going to be awful and I was sure to land in a ditch somewhere. It had to be, because this level of joy couldn't possibly last, could it?

Living in a state of joy does not mean that nothing bad ever happens to you, or that you'll never experience sadness ever again. It's the *way* you experience those emotions that will drastically change. The way you look at these obstacles that will change. This may be controversial, but as humans we often choose to suffer. There's nothing biologically in our bodies that requires us to suffer. Now I'm sure you're thinking of scenarios to combat this statement, and there are some tough ones, but the truth is we sometimes choose to suffer because it is fulfilling a need in us somewhere—a need to hold on to an attachment, a need to feel like we really "went through it" in order to deserve happiness again, a need to stay in our comfort zone, or perhaps even an excuse to hold ourselves back from living our most authentic lives. Once you choose to release the suffering and the fear, you have no excuses left as to why you're not living your life to its fullest degree. Forgiveness is for you, not for anyone else. It's a gift you give yourself. Closure is also a gift you can give yourself. Thinking you need closure from another person will just keep you in the same loop of seeking the external validation that we are trying to break here. YOU have the power to choose when you are done suffering, and that's okay if it isn't time yet.

The only way to change an old pattern is to become aware of it, and then consistently choose to break that pattern. We have the gift of free will. That also comes with a flip-side of taking accountability for our own happiness. Once you realize you have more control over your inner state of being, the freer you will feel. That domino effect of feeling free can lead to a multitude of positive life changes and alignments. It all starts with a choice, a commitment to yourself to allow joy in. It's okay to be scared. Stick with that choice of joy. The commitment to yourself will probably feel uncomfortable at first, like all new things, and that's okay. On the other side of discomfort hill are the rolling plains of freedom.

Why do we hold ourselves back?

In 99% of cases, it is usually out of fear. Fear of failure, fear of success (imposter syndrome), fear of sustainability, fear of change, or even fear of losing all sense of who you were. If you ask yourself enough WHY questions until you get to the bottom of it, the root is often fear-based. Fear can be crippling, yet elusive. It can protect you and keep you prisoner all in the same breath. I can think of many times I stayed too long out of fear, and I hold that version of me with such empathy now—knowing that the one thing I was scared to do was the one thing that would save my life and set me free. I'm a human being trying to figure all this life stuff out, just like you.

Even writing this book, I go through phases of it flowing effortlessly, and then there are days when I have zero desire to write and make myself feel guilty for it. I am no guru; I am no doctor; I don't have 80 certificates and licenses to tell you I'm an expert; I've never even written a book before. But I have lived every concept I write about and I have sat where you're sitting and I know how it feels. I'm writing this to the version of me that wished she had this book years ago, in hopes that it can be a friend when life seems dark, a helping hand shining the flashlight for you when you need it.

She stopped playing small.

She stopped acting un-tall.

For she could spin silk with syllables.

NOTES

Prompt: What would happen if it all worked out for you?

What does that look like? What fears come up when you think about everything actually turning out how you want it to? Sometimes, we are not afraid of failure, but of success.

• • • ● • ● • • •

Door 5: The Power of Belief

· · · · ● · ● ● · ·

The power of belief is the single most powerful tool we have. Your beliefs are the tools in your toolbox that shape the fabric of your reality. You can use these tools to build whatever life you desire. There have been countless studies about the placebo effect and your brain chemistry when you truly believe in something. It can change your whole life. That's why mirror work is so powerful: what you tell yourself in the mirror every day, you start to believe. Your words have power. That's why they call it spelling—they are spells. Your words can be soft and gentle, they can be sharp and hurtful, but they can also be used to elevate your being in a very real way.

Our ego always wants to protect us and is most concerned with our survival at a primal level. The things that allow us to grow in life are often scary. That fear is rooted in your ego, perceiving that moving outside your comfort zone will be unsafe. That is the constant battle between the ego and your consciousness to grow and move past challenges.

Think of your ego like a big scary guard dog. You need to learn to train your guard dog. This takes time, patience, and maybe some peanut butter, but it's doable. Enough care and love and patience can tame any dog; same with your ego. You can even name your ego Fluffy or Spot or Frank or whatever tickles your fancy. When it's acting up, and you don't want to do something because you're afraid of what people might think or afraid of change, talk to your guard dog. Give them a treat. Let them know whatever experience you are moving towards is safe to pass through.

The ego tries to protect our hearts and souls from hurt and rejection. Which is a good thing, and thank you ego, but you also can take your power back from that and realize that hurt and rejection are not lethal feelings. In fact, they might even strengthen you and teach you something you needed to learn. If we remove the fear surrounding the hurt and rejection, or even fear of being seen, and give our ego a bone, letting those feelings pass though, you will realize you *can* handle them. You can safely feel, and you will probably feel 1000x better after you do.

If you shift your limiting beliefs to ones that feel expansive, watch your life change unbelievably. I'll share a personal example. I have struggled with body image my whole life. I had an obsessive eating disorder by 7th grade and never thought I was skinny enough or fit enough to be accepted as having a beautiful body. I would look at my body with disdain and see all the parts I wanted to fix, and I'd get frustrated when I could never stick to a certain diet or exercise program to get to where I wanted to be physically. I used to look at people who loved their bodies and thought that there was no way that they actually loved them. There was no way they actually believed that. They must have been putting on a show of positivity. They had to be insecure and hate their belly fat rolls or their thick thighs, how could someone truly LOVE their body like that?

Well, I'm here to tell you I'm now one of those body-loving humans and I never in a million years thought I would get here. Every day isn't perfect, but loving yourself is a way of life. The changes started small, and I used the 5, 6, 7, 8 method from Door #1. I gave up on losing weight for specific occasions or events, stopped forcing myself into the gym because that's what I thought I had to do to be fit, and started changing the way I spoke to myself first, before changing the way I thought about myself. Trust me, I felt silly standing naked in front of the mirror and looking at my stomach and saying, "Thank you for digesting my food and I love you" out loud. I felt silly massaging it and trying to send it "loving energy." I felt silly for giving my thighs gratitude and for trying to look at my stretch marks from an artistic perspective. I had to catch myself and consciously change my speech when talking about myself. I try never to say "I look fat" or "I am gross" anymore. That doesn't mean I don't feel it sometimes, but I stopped saying it.

The more I did thank my body for working like the beautiful machine it is, and looking at my tiger stripes with love instead of disgust—things did start to change. I let go of having to work out a certain way and just tried to move my body as much as I could. This included dancing around the house, walking, flowy movement on my yoga mat, and even going to concerts just to dance. I didn't immediately become some body positivity warrior, but I started to feel less self-conscious. I started to feel prettier, more accepting of my body and myself. I start to carry myself with more confidence. I started to *believe* that I loved my body and that my body was beautiful. The funny thing is, when I let go of what I thought I *should* feel, and let flow what felt right *to me*, I ended up being the healthiest I've ever been. When I truly started loving my body, I also stopped feeding her crap and junk food and started caring about the chemicals and substances I was digesting. I started enjoying movement for how it made me feel. How it made me look was almost an after-effect. Once I shifted my belief from hating my body to loving my body, my life became more easily enjoyed and richer with color and beauty everywhere I turned.

This transformation can be applied to any limiting belief you have about yourself; it doesn't have to be a physical one. Maybe you think you're too talkative. Start working on believing that your voice is your power and thank yourself for the ability to use your words, which many people are too fearful to do. Maybe you think you're dumb. Start telling yourself you are smart in many unique ways and capable of learning new things. After a while, you will start to adopt that belief about yourself and find it easier to pick up information and try new activities. We all seem to be very good at believing negative things about ourselves and the world, but if we use that same power to start believing more positive things, we can change our realities, our bodies, and our minds.

The dark is just the dark.

That's it. It just is what is.

Contrast.

Love through the contrast,
for without it, there is no light.

NOTES

Prompt: Write 5 things that you love or that make you feel loved.

What about these things do you feel drawn to? How does it feel in your body when you think about these things?

• • • ● • ● • • •

Door 6: Finding Light in the Darkness

· · · ● · ● · ● · ·

When you think of JOY, you don't think of darkness, do you?

They are often two sides of the same coin. They are old friends, that often visit one another. There will always be heavy shit going on. That is a guarantee. How would you know the difference between joy and sadness if one did not exist without the other?

"The most powerful emotions are the ones that hold the duality of our existence and words just can't quite do them justice." — Reta Grace Moretti

Ying and Yang: They're seemingly opposite, yet hold pieces and parts of each other, and fit together in harmony. For example, as I am writing this book about finding joy, my best friend found out she had stage 4 ovarian cancer and passed away all in the course of less than 2 weeks.

Now you may think, how tragic and awful (first it was the dog, now best friends too! Come on, Kath), and you are very correct. However, I also choose to see the yang in all of this. I can't help but notice the immense outpour of love and healing she was a catalyst for. People that were too afraid to feel their emotions and talk about their feelings to anyone are now openly sharing and releasing years of trauma mirrored by this collective experience, leaving them feeling lighter and freer. She's given me the gift of amplifying my own intuitive powers and helping facilitate for others. She helped me learn how to be a crossing guard for those passing on from this world in the most beautiful way. She's even helping me write this book! If we take our human fear-based scarcity emotions away from our ego, and look at situations from a love-based perspective, I promise you you can always find a glimmer of light in the dark—and often it's more than just a spark, it's a whole fireworks display.

We all hold grief. Whether it is the grief over the loss of a loved one, the grief of the atrocities happening in the world, or the often overlooked grief of an old version of yourself or situation you are moving on from and no longer need. Grief is like surfing: Sometimes you're paddling out. Sometimes you're just preparing to stand up. Sometimes you're riding the best wave and feel the sun on your face. Sometimes you are just sitting on your board observing. And sometimes you wipe the F out. (P.S. I don't know how to surf, either.) But you always come up out of the water and take a breath again no matter what happens in the current. That breath is the spark. It is our human ability to time and time again remain resilient in the face of chaos.

Many people deal with dark, depressing, sad, or toxic thoughts and feelings. Think of them as just shitty guests in the Airbnb of your mind. Sometimes these Airbnb guests only stay a night, but sometimes they book an extended stay. Either way, they will always leave eventually. Here's how I like to look at them:

1. Don't judge yourself for feeling/thinking. Take the SELF out of it, and try to separate the thought or feeling and not internalize it as a part of who you are. Meet them with curiosity and kindness, like you would a hurt puppy on the side of the road.

2. Think of your thoughts as fuel for your brain. You want to feed your brain healthy fuel if at all possible, the majority of the time. If you catch yourself in a toxic thought pattern, say out loud to yourself, "We don't think like this anymore." That gives your brain a moment to pause and acknowledge that you are intentionally rewiring those neurons that were previously firing together. Do this as often as you need to. (Thank you, Ashlee Shostrom, for making a TikTok on this years ago that stuck in my brain!)

3. Hello Darkness, My Old Friend. Ask the darkness questions. Pause, and say, "Hey girl (boy, unicorn, snake, whatever you want), hey, what are

you here to teach me? Thank you for coming to deliver me a lesson, I am open to learning." You can also say, "Thank you for coming to deliver a lesson to me, but show me this curriculum in a different way." You may be surprised what shifts you start to notice in your overall well-being and anxiety levels.

4. MOVE. Energy is stored in different organs and areas of your body. Move your body. You can jump up and down, dance, run, box, do yoga, hump the air for all I care—just MOVE. Too much compacted stored energy has the potential to become unsafe for your body.

You may be surprised at how quickly you can start to feel lighter, feel joy, notice the small miracles, just from simple shifts in how you look at darkness. Besides, the most colorful light is always seen best in the darkness. So let your brain rave a little.

Love is limitless.

There is an ocean of joy.

You get to decide how much joy you let into your life by the size of the container you bring to the shoreline.

NOTES

Prompt: Think about the limitless ocean and draw a doodle or swirl or anything that feels good to scribble on this page.

Let your pen flow however it wants, without judgment or form.

• • • ● • ● • • •

Door 7: Find Rhythm in the Spin

• • • ● • ● • • •

T he only constant in life is change. The world keeps turning. No matter what is going on in our personal lives, the spin never stops. Sometimes it's too much to sit still, too much to take a moment to meditate or sit in nature; you may feel too worked up and that's okay. We can work with that. Allow the spin. Allow it to move you. Even if you sit down for a moment and close your eyes, move in circular motions with your body, hands on your knees and give in to the spin—find its rhythm. We put so much energy into resistance: resistance to what is, resistance to our next chapters in life, resistance to change. What would happen if you just allowed the spin?

Allow the spin to drill you all the way down and ground you. Slowly the spin will get smaller and smaller. Every tornado has stillness in the eye. The world can be spinning all around us, throwing shit in the air and you feel like you're in a whirlwind, but there is ALWAYS going to be an eye of stillness.

Think of a jet ski. If you resist in the opposite direction out of fear of falling, you fall faster and the jet ski is thrown off balance. If you lean into the curve instead and flow *with* it, you will remain afloat. Same goes with life. If you can't sit still, don't. Sit unstill. Move your body. Allow your mind to wander if it does, and just observe that. Eventually, you will realize you are remaining afloat and might even find gratitude for that float.

Whenever I really want something, I've found I never get it in a state of wanting. That is coming from a state of lack. It's okay to desire more in life, but instead of wanting it from a state of lack, try to envision what you feel like when you already have it. It's already in your river of life, you just haven't floated down to it quite yet. Coming from that state of have-ness creates a stronger pull towards it.

Some people like to call this manifestation. I personally think that word is overused and often misguided, but its principal nature stands. Once you feel what it is like to be in that state of having whatever it is you want, here's the hardest part but the quickest way to get it: set it and forget it. Let it go. Let go the need of wanting it to happen and start to look at all the things you have and find things to be thankful for in the current present state of your life, knowing that everything is still in your river and on its way. When you fully and truly let go of it, it's absolutely wild how quickly it can actually materialize for you. I've experienced this happening time and time again. I'll give you an example.

I was working in corporate marketing for ten years. Towards the end, although I loved my team with all my heart, my work felt so soulless. I got anxiety every night, knowing how many meetings I had the next day and how much energy I would have to expend doing things that are somewhat meaningless to the greater good of the world. That started to eat away at me. I set an intention that I no longer wanted to work in corporate America. I wanted to help people heal and inspire people and connect with humans on a greater scale and be able to support myself through doing this work—however the details looked didn't matter. I wrote this in my journals, felt what it felt like to live that life, and even thanked the universe for what a beautiful life I had with all of these elements even though I didn't have it yet. I did this often, and got comfortable with feeling this reality.

Here was the hardest part. Instead of thinking about wanting a different life every day and being miserable at my job and wishing I could escape, I shifted my mindset about my *current* situation. Every day I would wake up and think about how grateful I was to even have a job to pay my bills. I made a list of all the things about the job that DID ignite me and that I enjoyed. Most of those things had to do with connecting to the people there and creativity. Then I would look at all my meetings and think, what aspects of my attitude about them can I shift in order to focus on the aspects that did bring me joy, i.e., connection and creativity. How could I arrange my projects to add even 1% more joy into my day instead of being so negative about it?

When I started doing this and shifted my mindset about my situation, I started feeling less anxiety and less stress. It didn't fix everything and make me love my job suddenly, but the acceptance of my current state of affairs became my solace. I had the power to find joy wherever I wanted. That in itself was a beautiful realization; that I didn't need this next chapter before I was happy. I didn't have to wait to feel happiness or joy. I gave myself the permission to feel it right now, in this moment, no matter the circumstances.

When I did this, it was then only a few weeks before I was freed from my corporate job with a nice severance. I realized the universe had been setting me up for success the whole year with things I thought were mishaps (like my house flooding), actually giving me the cushion to move onto my next chapter.

At the beginning of 2024 I was stuck in 10 meetings a day doing endless PowerPoints, disheartened and pondering my existence. By the end of 2024, I was sitting on my couch in my own place, on my own schedule, writing you this book and pouring my heart out doing what I love—connecting with humans. That's how quickly your life can change. It is possible, because I did it. I'm not an heiress, I don't have a rich husband paying my bills (congrats if you do though, no shade here sis), I didn't have to sell my soul to anyone, and I'm doing this. I'm living a joyful life. I'm just a girl from Kalamazoo, Michigan, who lived with constant curiosity and an open mind—followed her heart and intuition to the utmost degree, and refused to settle. If I can do it, so can you.

Now it's up to you. You are the expert of your own life. You have the responsibility to feel joy, it's no one else's to gift to give you. Yes, it's work.

Anything worth it is, but it's not as hard as you think it's going to be—I promise you that. Once you start to notice the little sparks of joy, they multiply like fireworks. Remember, where your focus goes, energy flows. If you practice the art of noticing joy, you will be astounded how much more joy you notice and how much gets drawn to you.

People ask me what I think the purpose of life is. As I mentioned earlier, I believe we're in somewhat of a soul school. There's all different levels of souls here learning various areas of study. Some lives have different curriculums and challenges to overcome, and sometimes that seems unfair. Personally, I try not to judge the fabric of the universe and these cosmic decisions that are made. What I do think, is if you use your free will to commit to giving and receiving love and amplifying that frequency of love in all that you do—even with the shit thrown at you and life obstacles in your way—your soul will grow and find uncircumstantial peace. You will start to radiate that feeling back out at a level that will help others feel it too, and hopefully inspire them to seek that loving peaceful state of being, which in turn will help heal the earth itself and all the beings on it.

I can't heal you. You are the healer of your own wounds. I simply have the honor of holding a mirror for you to look at your life in perhaps a different way and begin to heal yourself. That is an honor I do not take for granted. At this point we feel like friends, so I want to let you know I'm proud of you. I'm proud of you for even picking up this book and having the intention of wanting to better your existence. That in itself is a huge step, even if this book just sits on your shelf and you look at it every day as a reminder of that intention.

Everything happens in due time. Try to IN-Joy the process, the journey. Don't judge yourself too much, we're all just figuring it out. The magic is, that now we're figuring it out *together*.

Lead with Love.

Love, Always.

Love, Anyways.

Love is NEVER wasted.

NOTES

Prompt: Free write any words, thoughts, or phrases that come to your mind after reading all of this information.

This can be anything: colors, street names, the weather, things you can see around you, names, something you like to do, anything. Maybe even write one thing you learned in this book. See what comes through and have fun. You earned it. IN-Joy.

• • • • • • • • • •

Acknowledgements

• • • ● • ● • • •

Joey Ives- My Mother, My Ultimate Mirror

Thank you for always being my biggest cheerleader and grandest support system. You have always encouraged me to be my most authentic self (even when it didn't necessarily align with your beliefs) and for that support I am eternally grateful. Thank you for showing me you can be inspired at any age, being an ultimate pillar of courage, bravery, and unconditional love. My love and respect for you as a woman, wife, friend, and mother continues to grow each and every day. I love you.

Peter Ives- My Father, My Earth Angel

Being loved by you has been such an honor. Going through this journey of life with you has taught me a multitude of lessons and I am so grateful for you imparting your eternal wisdom to me. This journey of dementia has brought us together in a new level of unconditional love and I cherish each moment we get to spend together. I love you.

My Best Friends- My Soul Sisters

I could not have written this book without your love, support, encouragement, laughter, tears, and joy. Thank you for teaching me a deeper level of happiness and gratitude than I ever thought possible. Thank you for being mirrors. Thank you for all the times we have spent being, rather than doing. Thank you for helping me heal my wounds. Thank you for sending flowers when I needed them. Thank you being in my corner and for raising the friendship bar. I love you endlessly.

The Men of My Life- Mirrors, Lessons, and Protectors

Relationships & friends, old and new, who have shown me what it's like to feel safe and appreciated, my heart is always with you. The challenging ones that didn't work out have gifted me the most valuable lessons and transformations, which I could not have written this book without experiencing. Forgiveness is a gift you give yourself, and I am grateful for all of you. Thank you for aiding in my journey to joy.

MB - You have become the steady rock through my creative waves, igniting the spark that kept me going. Thank you for never making me feel like I'm too much, and for loving my muchness.

My Lilly Girl- My Soul Dog Forever

I know you won't be able to read this without opposable thumbs, unless they gave you those over the rainbow bridge, but thank you for being the catalyst to the most transformative chapter of my life. You taught me patience, love, devotion, joy, responsibility, grief, pain, acceptance, and connection like no other. I know you keep bringing me new doggo friends too, and I love you for it. Run wild sister, you're free.

My Mentors- My Teachers in Divine Timing

I am so grateful to a handful of humans that I could not have started or finished this book without. If you're thinking you might be one of them, I'm sure that you are.

Sasha, you have been paramount to my spiritual journey and personal growth. I cannot express what gratitude I hold for your soul. It runs deep.

Kayla, Mariet Kay herself, this book would not be here now without your guidance. Thank you for so generously sharing your publishing wisdom with me.

The support from you both gave me the clarity, courage, and confidence I needed to bring this book into the world.

Ellen Todras, my wonderful editor- thank you and Dhyani for being a part of this journey with me.

Laura Huertas, the Thelma to my Louise, the Bad to my Bunny- Thank you for the beautiful photograph that brought my back cover to life, and truly made me feel like an author. The way you capture life through photography is art and never ceases to inspire me. Adriane Leigh, my cosmic twin, thank you for always letting us play in your studio and inspiring me to create with my inner-child. You both bring so much beauty to my life, and I am so grateful.

To the many other mentors, healers, and teachers I've had in between- thank you for proving collaboration is greater than competition.

A Love Note From Kathleen

• • • ● • ● • • •

To My Readers,

I want to say thank you. Out of all the books in the world, you chose this one. Or perhaps, it chose you. Either way, I am deeply honored. Your presence here means more than you know.

I hope *7 Ways to Live IN-Joy Today* sparked something within you, or at the very least painted a smile across your face. If it did, I would be so grateful if you shared a review. Hearing your reflections means the world to me, and your words might just help someone else discover the joy you found too.

And if you feel the nudge, send me a note. Magic happens in connection: hello@kathleenives.com or DM @kathleenives_

www.ingramcontent.com/pod-product-compliance
Lightning Source LLC
Chambersburg PA
CBHW021118130626
46554CB00002B/748